BASKETBALL LEGENDS

Kareem Abdul-Jabbar
Charles Barkley
Larry Bird
Kobe Bryant
Wilt Chamberlain
Clyde Drexler
Julius Erving
Patrick Ewing
Kevin Garnett
Anfernee Hardaway
Tim Hardaway
The Head Coaches
Grant Hill
Juwan Howard
Allen Iverson
Magic Johnson
Michael Jordan
Shawn Kemp
Jason Kidd
Reggie Miller
Alonzo Mourning
Hakeem Olajuwon
Shaquille O'Neal
Gary Payton
Scottie Pippen
David Robinson
Dennis Rodman
John Stockton
Keith Van Horn
Antoine Walker
Chris Webber

CHELSEA HOUSE PUBLISHERS

BASKETBALL LEGENDS

ANTOINE WALKER

Donald Hunt

Introduction by
Chuck Daly

CHELSEA HOUSE PUBLISHERS
Philadelphia

Produced by Combined Publishing, Inc.

CHELSEA HOUSE PUBLISHERS

Editor in Chief: Stephen Reginald
Managing Editor: James Gallagher
Production Manager: Pamela Loos
Art Director: Sara Davis
Director of Photography: Judy L. Hasday
Senior Production Editor: Lisa Chippendale
Publishing Coordinator: James McAvoy
Cover Design and Digital Illustration: Keith Trego

Cover Photos: AP/Wide World Photos

The Chelsea House World Wide Web site address is
http://www.chelseahouse.com

First Printing

1 3 5 7 9 8 6 4 2

Library of Congress Cataloging-in-Publication Data

Hunt, Donald, 1955 -
      Antoine Walker / Donald Hunt.
        p.   cm. — (Basketball legends)
      Includes bibliographical references and index.
      Summary: A biography of the Kentucky Wildcats star
      who was picked by the Boston Celtics in the NBA
      draft in 1996.
      ISBN 0-7910-5008-4 (hc)
      1. Walker, Antoine, 1976-   —Juvenile literature.
      2.Basketball players—United States—Biography—
      Juvenile literature.
      [1. Walker, Antoine, 1976- . 2. Basketball players.
      3. Afro-Americans—Biography.] I. Title. II. Series.
      GV884.W25H86 1998
      796.323'092—dc21
      [b]   98-45048
                                     CIP
                                     AC

CONTENTS

BECOMING A BASKETBALL LEGEND

Chuck Daly

What does it take to be a basketball superstar? Two of the three things it takes are easy to spot. Any great athlete must have excellent skills and tremendous dedication. The third quality needed is much harder to define, or even put in words. Others call it leadership or desire to win, but I'm not sure that explains it fully. This third quality relates to the athlete's thinking process, a certain mentality and work ethic. One can coach athletic skills, and while few superstars need outside influence to help keep them dedicated, it is possible for a coach to offer some well-timed words in order to keep that athlete fully motivated. But a coach can do no more than appeal to a player's will to win; how much that player is then capable of ensuring victory is up to his own internal workings.

In recent times, we have been fortunate to have seen some of the best to play the game. Larry Bird, Magic Johnson, and Michael Jordan had all three components of superstardom in full measure. They brought their teams to numerous championships, and made the players around them better. (They also made their coaches look smart.)

I myself coached a player who belongs in that class, Isiah Thomas, who helped lead the Detroit Pistons to consecutive NBA crowns. Isiah is not tall—he's just over six feet—but he could do whatever he wanted with the ball. And what he wanted to do most was lead and win.

All the players I mentioned above and those whom this series will chronicle are tremendously gifted athletes, but for the most part, you can't play professional basketball at all unless you have excellent skills. And few players get to stay on their team unless they are willing to dedicate themselves to improving their talents even more, learning about their opponents, and finding a way to join with their teammates and win.

It's that third element that separates the good player from the superstar, the memorable players from the legends of the game. Superstars know when to take over the game. If the situation calls for a defensive stop, the superstars stand up and do it. If the situation calls for a key pass, they make it. And if the situation calls for a big shot, they want the ball. They don't want the ball simply because of their own glory or ego. Instead they know—and their teammates know—that they are the ones who can deliver, regardless of the pressure.

The words "legend" and "superstar" are often tossed around without real meaning. Taking a hard look at some of those who truly can be classified as "legends" can provide insight into the things that brought them to that level. All of them developed their legacy over numerous seasons of play, even if certain games will always stand out in the memories of those who saw them. Those games typically featured amazing feats of all-around play. No matter how great the fans thought the superstars were, these players were capable of surprising the fans, their opponents, and occasionally even themselves. The desire to win took over, and with their dedication and athletic skills already in place, they were capable of the most astonishing achievements.

CHUCK DALY, now the head coach of the Orlando Magic, guided the Detroit Pistons to two straight NBA championships, in 1989 and 1990. He earned a gold medal as coach of the 1992 U.S. Olympic basketball team—the so-called "Dream Team"—and was inducted into the Pro Basketball Hall of Fame in 1994.

MAKING THE
ALL-STAR TEAM

Antoine Walker didn't get a chance to put on a spectacular show in his first NBA All-Star game. He only shot two for eight from the field, scoring four points, while handing out three assists. But Walker did come off the bench to throw a perfect behind-the-back pass to Indiana's Reggie Miller for a layup. Walker's pass made the highlights of just about every national sports show across the country.

The Boston Celtics' second-year forward helped the East defeat the West, 135-114, at New York's Madison Square Garden.

For a player who is known for his flashy style, Walker took a somewhat laid-back approach to the All-Star game. The fans didn't see much of the high-stepping, long-range shooting, and no-look passes they're used to seeing in Boston Fleet Center.

Walker was clearly just happy to be there. He was happy to be a part of a winning team

Antoine Walker maneuvers past the defense of the Utah Jazz' Greg Foster.

that featured Michael Jordan.

When you think of the great young players in the NBA, Antoine Walker's name comes to mind right away. That's why the NBA coaches selected him to play in the All-Star game. Walker joined a distinguished list of former University of Kentucky stars—Cliff Hagan, Ralph Beard, Adrian Smith, and Dan Issel—who played in the All-Star Game over the years. Issel was the last Kentucky alumni to participate in an All-Star Game, playing in the 1977 matchup.

Walker was the sixth player chosen in the 1996 NBA draft, and in just two seasons he was named to the All-Rookie Team and to the All-Star Team.

Walker was selected as a reserve on the East team with Jayson Williams of the New Jersey Nets, Glen Rice of the Charlotte Hornets, Tim Hardaway of the Miami Heat, Reggie Miller and Rick Smits of the Indiana Pacers, and Steve Smith of the Atlanta Hawks. He was the first Celtic to be chosen for the All-Star game since the late Reggie Lewis made the team in 1992.

"I think if this team had won 12 games or 10 games or eight games, Antoine wouldn't have made it," Boston coach Rick Pitino told the *Boston Herald*. He was Walker's coach at the University of Kentucky before joining the Celtics. "But because we've had some early success, he did make it. We've showed a lot of improvement for a team that's coming off 15 wins, and he's the biggest reason why."

Walker, a 6'9", 245-pound forward, was aver-

Walker drives the ball down the court in a "coast-to-coast" move that helped him make the 1998 NBA All-Star team.

Antoine Walker soon found himself being mentioned with former Celtics greats such as Larry Bird (above) and Robert Parish.

aging 21.9 points and 10.5 rebounds a game prior to the All-Star break. He felt he had a good chance to make the All-Star team, but he also believed his teammates played a major role in helping him get to the game in New York.

"There was a lot of pressure," Walker told the *Boston Herald*. "This was the first year I felt I should make it, but you don't know what's going to happen. I didn't know if I had the respect around the league yet. It was kind of wearing on my mind, because you figure if you don't make it this year, you might not make it next year."

Most basketball experts saw a great deal of talent in Walker during his rookie year. He led the Celtics in 1996-97 in scoring (17.5 ppg), rebounds (9.0 rpg), and blocked shots (53) and was the only Celtic to appear in all 82 games.

His second season, Walker left no doubts about his basketball skills. He was able to put the ball on the floor, shoot from the three-point range, rebound, and play good defense.

Though just 22, Walker was one of the most versatile players in the NBA. He was capable of playing small forward, power forward, center, and even shooting guard. He showed amazing skills for a player who should have been a senior at Kentucky.

In his second NBA season, Walker put together some impressive statistics, catching the attention of many coaches and players throughout the league. Some of the highlights included:

* Walker's game-high 38 points, 11 rebounds, 6 assists, and 3 steals against the Charlotte Hornets.
* His third career triple-double, with 27 points, 14 rebounds, and 10 assists, in a 107-96 win over the Houston Rockets.

Rick Pitino, head coach of the Boston Celtics, poses with three of his players: Ron Mercer (5), Antoine Walker (8), and Chauncey Billups (4).

* A team-high 32 points, 10 rebounds, and 5 assists in a 106-99 victory over the Milwaukee Bucks.
* A career-high 49 points, shooting 21 of 36 from the field, and 12 rebounds in a losing effort against the Washington Wizards.

With such spectacular performances, Walker was an easy pick for the All-Star team. He had a way of making everything look easy. Sometimes it was hard to tell whether he was even sweating.

He moved so smoothly and swiftly on the court. There were games where Walker grabbed a rebound, put the ball on the floor, and took it all the way to the basket.

That's called going coast-to-coast. That's All-Star talent.

"He's just scratching the surface of his potential," Pitino told *Basketball Digest*. "He is going to get a lot stronger, become a better shooter, a better finisher, and more of a leader. He has a passion for the game, and that's what makes him so good."

Walker, the Celtics' team captain, had his name mentioned with such former Boston greats as Larry Bird, Kevin McHale, and Robert Parish. These players were All Stars and a major reason for the Celtics' success during the 1980s. They won NBA championships in '81, '84, and '87.

While the Celtics during Walkers' first two seasons weren't as strong as those championship teams, the team did have some fine young players, including Walker's Kentucky teammates, Ron Mercer and Walter McCarty. McCarty and Mercer gave Walker a chance to shine. And McCarty and Mercer, like Walker, were expected to grow and improve each year. The future looked bright for the Celtics.

Improvement was the key word. Walker had to get better each year in order to keep his All-Star status. He had to continue to improve other areas of his game, like foul shots and defense.

If he continued to work on his game, he would have a regular spot on the NBA All-Star team. He would also become one of the best players in Celtic history.

As part of the plan for Walker to improve, Coach Pitino wanted him to build up his body. He felt Walker could become another Karl Malone in terms of his physique.

"I feel Antoine can develop his body like Karl Malone's," Pitino told the *Boston Globe*. "He can be 265 pounds."

That was a 20-pound gain. Pitino believed Walker would dominate the game physically with a bigger and stronger body. He didn't think Walker would lose any of his legendary quickness with the extra weight. Walker was quicker than most power forwards and stronger than most small forwards.

The coach also wanted to see Walker shoot more consistently from 17 feet, cutting down on the number of three-pointers. That way, his field-goal percentage would climb above 40 percent.

No one knew more about Walker's ability than Pitino. He knew how to push the ex-Wildcat to become a better player. "I truly believe this, not only because I recruited him in college, but I think Antoine Walker is one of the future stars," Pitino said. "He sort of reminds me of when I used to watch Magic Johnson, watch a 6'9" person who can do so many things with the ball. I don't mean to put that type of pressure on Antoine to even compare someone to Magic, but he does the things that remind me of Magic. He handles the ball, finds people open and when the shot clock is winding, he'll create an instant offense for you. He can also pound it inside and make great moves in the interior. He's without question a star right now."

2

GROWING UP IN CHICAGO

Antoine Devon Walker grew up in Chicago. His father, Dennis Seats, worked in the Chicago Park District, and his mother, Diane Walker, worked for the Cook County Sheriff's Department.

His mother said Walker's father left home when he was five, according to the *Hartford Courant*. Walker said his father wasn't a major factor in his life, but he doesn't harbor any bitterness toward him.

Antoine is one of six children, including brothers Tobias, Darius, and Jarvis and sisters Twyanna and Kenesha. While he enjoyed dancing and bowling for fun, sports is in his blood; he is related to former major league baseball player Chico Walker.

But baseball isn't Walker's game. Basketball is. And basketball was what kept Walker out of trouble as a kid. Walker was raised in a very rough part of the city, according to Mike Curta,

Recruited by many colleges, Walker chose to play basketball for the Kentucky Wildcats in order to work with Coach Rick Pitino.

the Mt. Carmel High School basketball coach.

"There's routinely gunfire across the boulevard, and the kids can identify the type of gun by the sound of the gunfire," Curta told the *Hartford Courant.*

Walker was a tremendous player at Mt. Carmel High School who gave his all for the team. Once, even though he smashed a glass door with his left hand during halftime of a basketball game, Walker played the rest of the game with a bloody bandage on his hand. He didn't leave to get stitches until after the game was over.

Curta was always impressed with his skills.

"He was a good kid, who I thought early on in high school was done harm by everyone jumping on the bandwagon, saying he was going to be the next Michael Jordan," said Curta. "That quote was in the paper when he was 14. When you're the best player on the floor, you can get away with some things."

Chicago has produced a lot of great basketball players: Maurice Cheeks, Terry Cummings, Nick Anderson, Hersey Hawkins, and Isiah Thomas, Walker's boyhood idol.

Walker is certainly in that class. The man nicknamed "Toine" scored more than 2,000 points in high school and played a lot of summer basketball against NBA players like Tim Hardaway of the Miami Heat, Nick Anderson of the Orlando Magic, Randy Brown of the Chicago Bulls, and others.

Walker believed, however, that his high-stepping style, not to mention his flair for dramatics in key games, may have hurt him a little in the eyes of some college recruiters.

And according to an article in the *Chicago Sun-Times,* many people thought Walker was a

Antoine dunks the ball now wearing the Kentucky Wildcat uniform. Coach Pitino called him one of the two best players he's ever recruited.

very selfish player. His attitude was the reason he wasn't chosen as Chicago's Catholic League player of the year. There were a number of coaches who wouldn't recruit him because they thought he was uncontrollable.

Walker reportedly was recruited by several major college basketball programs, however, including Michigan, Illinois, and the University of Nevada, Las Vegas.

Walker had received plenty of glory playing in Chicago. He was quite a legend on the playgrounds. But Walker felt he needed to play college basketball away from his hometown. There was a lot of pressure for him to stay home and play for the University of Illinois. Walker's mother, Diane, was a little surprised when he decided to go to Kentucky. She wasn't too familiar with the school's winning basketball program, but she said that was where her son wanted to go all along.

"I didn't know much about Kentucky," Diane told the *Chicago Sun-Times*. "But Antoine, he knew everything about Kentucky. That's where he always had his eye."

Walker was more than happy to get away from the pressures of playing at home.

"Basketball is everything in Chicago," Walker told the *Houston Chronicle*. "People always nag you to talk about the game. It's all in good fun, but you don't need that every game. People expect 40 points or whatever and 20 rebounds every night. I needed to get away from that."

So he decided to play for the Kentucky Wildcats.

"I just love the press and run style of Kentucky," Walker told the *Chicago Sun-Times*. "That was the main thing. If I'm in the spotlight less, that's fine. Everybody gets their own special attention. Because we win. When you win 30-odd games and have a chance to win it all, everybody gets some glory."

"When you are from a big city, you play against top competition," Walker told the *Advocate Messenger*. "That showed me I could play with anybody. I have a high confidence level. I'm not cocky, just confident. Some people don't understand the difference. . . .

"In high school I wasn't much of a practice player. I know I have to turn into one here [at Kentucky]. In high school, I was more of a game player because I knew I was going to start. I was never challenged in high school. I didn't have many games where anybody could check me. I was out of control at times in high school. That's one reason I wanted to come here. I need the discipline coach Pitino has. I play with a lot of emotion, but I'll play the way coach Pitino wants."

"Everybody told me, 'Don't recruit him,' " Kentucky's Pitino told the *Chicago Sun-Times*. "Fortunately, I listened to my assistant coaches. The

Walker's abilities on the court would impress his new coaches and team-mates alike at Kentucky.

two best players I've been able to recruit have been Jamal Mashburn and Antoine Walker. And everybody told me not to recruit either one."

As a youngster, Walker's favorite basketball players were Isiah Thomas and Magic Johnson. Of course, Thomas, like Walker, was a great high school basketball star in Chicago.

Walker picked stellar role models for his own basketball career. Thomas and Johnson were

Magic Johnson, here leaping for the ball against the Blazers, was one of Walker's childhood role models.

two of the greatest players to ever play in the NBA. And before that, both players won NCAA championships. Thomas led Indiana to a national title in 1981. Johnson guided Michigan State to a national championship in 1979.

In the NBA, Johnson helped the Los Angeles Lakers win five NBA championships, in 1980, 1982, 1985, 1987, and 1988. Thomas helped the Detroit Pistons capture back-to-back titles in 1989 and 1990.

Walker seems to be moving on the same track. Like Thomas and Johnson, whose college teams won national championships, Walker would be an important part of the Kentucky Wildcats' NCAA championship team.

3

THE NCAA
CHAMPIONSHIP

When Antoine Walker arrived at the University of Kentucky in 1994 as a high school All-American from Chicago, he knew the Wildcats had enough talent to win a national championship his first year in Lexington, Kentucky. As a freshman, Walker was extremely talented, but inconsistent, too. He was selected most valuable player in the Southeastern Conference tournament, a highlight of his first season. But Walker failed to sparkle in the NCAA tournament. In fact, he had a miserable game against North Carolina in the Southeast Regional, scoring just two points.

Walker didn't have big numbers most of his freshman year. He averaged 7.8 points and 4.5 rebounds a game. The next year, he put together a great season averaging 15.2 points and 8.4 rebounds a game, while leading Kentucky to a national title and a sensational 34-2 record, the second best winning record in school history.

No other Kentucky team had ever won 27

Antoine goes for the score past Virginia Tech's Ace Custis in the NCAA Midwest Regional championship.

25

Massachusetts center Marcus Camby, left, goes for the rebound against Kentucky's Antoine Walker.

straight games in one season. The Wildcats also became the first team in 40 years to go through the Southeastern Conference regular season with an unblemished record, 16-0.

In addition, the Wildcats regained the honor as the winningest team in college basketball. Kentucky had the most NCAA tournament victories (70), the most NCAA tournament appearances (37), and the team won national titles under three different head coaches.

The team came a long way from where it was in 1989. That year, Rick Pitino took over the program, which had been placed on probation for two years by the NCAA.

There were a few rough spots along the way to East Rutherford and the national title.

After the Wildcats had fought back from being down 11 points in their first victory against Maryland in the Tip Off Classic, it was off to the Great Eight in Auburn Hills, Michigan. With its preseason No. 1 ranking still intact, the team was bursting with confidence. Against Maryland, Mark Pope tallied 26 points and yanked down six boards to snare most valuable player honors, while Tony Delk poured in 19 of 21 points in the second half. The two appeared to be a great inside-outside combo.

But against Massachusetts (UMass), the Wildcats really struggled. UMass center Marcus Camby emerged as the early leader for college basketball's player of the year honors after depositing 32 points, nine rebounds, and five blocked shots. Moreover, the Minutemen came away with a 92-82 victory, knocking Kentucky from its No. 1 spot while giving the Wildcats a .500 mark after two games. For Pitino, it was a blessing in disguise.

"If we win that game, we don't win the national championship," Pitino said after winning his first NCAA championship four months later. "That loss taught us more about our team than any win on our schedule."

The team certainly learned its lesson quite well. Delk would have to play the shooting guard spot for the team to succeed. Anthony Epps

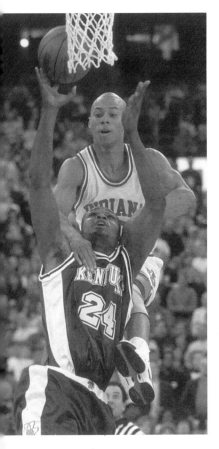

An intentional foul was called on this move by Indiana's Sherron Wilkerson as he climbs the back of Antoine Walker.

would need to step up his game as the starting point guard. Walker, who missed the start that night, would not miss another. And Derek Anderson would have to get his playing time.

When more than 41,000 fans filled the RCA Dome in Indianapolis the following weekend, it was a new-and-improved Kentucky team. While the bench played sparingly, Walker and Anderson did not. Walker was almost perfect, shooting 10 for 12 from the field and grabbing seven rebounds as he finished with 24 points. Anderson finished with 18 points and three assists.

For the third straight contest, Kentucky had its third different high scorer. And for the remainder of the season, no player averaged more than 27 minutes per game in the Wildcats' balanced attack. Eleven different Wildcats tallied 9.3 minutes or more per outing. The reserves were so productive that they finished the season averaging 31.4 points, 13.9 rebounds and 8.6 assists per game.

Still, after three games, Kentucky had not quite become what Pitino was expecting. And it would not happen right away.

A 12-point home-court victory over Wisconsin-Green Bay was discounted, with Kentucky criticized for being flat in the second half after leading 35-13 late in the opening period. In the next game, using his fifth different starting line-up in five games, Pitino watched Georgia Tech freshman Stephon Marbury display his NBA potential by dumping 17 first-half points in Rupp Arena. But the freshman was held scoreless in the second half as the Wildcats overcame a three-

Georgia Tech's Stephon Marbury tries to drive past the defense of Antoine Walker, December 9, 1995.

point deficit at the break to win 83-60. The Yellow Jackets scored only 19 points in the second half.

After spanking Morehead State, 96-32, in a game in which Kentucky tied the Rupp Arena records for blocks (16) and rebounds (62), it was on to Louisville's Freedom Hall to face Marshall. Kentucky silenced the Thundering Herd, crushing former Kentucky assistant coach Billy Donovan's team with a 32-2 spurt in a 6:36 stretch of the first half. After leading 70-49 at the midway point, the fourth-ranked Wildcats cruised to a 118-99 victory.

Next was Louisville. The much-anticipated game was seen by a record crowd of 24,340. Delk was unstoppable, finishing with 30 points, six rebounds, two assists and two steals. Meanwhile, Walker, Pope and Walter McCarty combined to hold Louisville big man Samaki Walker to 17 points, forcing the center into six turnovers.

After Christmas, the Wildcats were off to New York City for the ECAC Holiday Festival, where Kentucky defeated Rider and Iona to win the tournament in Madison Square Garden. Delk continued his great play, scoring 24 points in the opener and 29 in the final to take home MVP honors. He also earned the SEC's Player of the Week award, the only time a Wildcat won the honor the entire season.

With the start of January, it was off to South Carolina, where the Wildcats outscored the Gamecocks, 50-26, in the second half to pick up their first road win, 89-60. After a victory at home over Ole Miss, it was on to Mississippi State for a showdown with the 12th-ranked Bulldogs. Mississippi State had a tough time as Kentucky forced 28 turnovers to pick up a

Kentucky's Walker jumps for a layup above the head of Florida's Greg Williams in the SEC tournament.

74-56 victory. For the first time, the question came up: Could Kentucky go undefeated in the conference?

After beating Tennessee in Lexington, the team went to Baton Rouge to face Louisiana State University. When the Wildcats and the Tigers battle, it is usually entertaining, but few had ever seen an offensive display like what Kentucky provided in the first half. They set a school and league record with 86 first-half points. Kentucky shot 67.3 percent from the field in the first half, forced 21 turnovers and grabbed 16 steals. The final score: Kentucky over LSU, 129-97.

The Wildcats continued their scoring binge by tallying 124 points in their next game against Texas Christian University, setting a school record for most points in back-to-back games with 253.

But if the Wildcats were going to have a rough time, it would be at Georgia. A former Kentucky assistant coach, now the Georgia head coach, was already building a solid program and the fans were ready for an upset. Yet, Delk would step up again. The senior guard scored 29 points on 11 for 19 shooting from the field. Allen Edwards also rose to the occasion, hitting clutch baskets twice in the final minutes, with the lead down to one point. The performances helped Kentucky secure a 82-77 win.

Pitino's team continued to play well in the final month of the regular season, picking up its second win over South Carolina, as well as victories over Florida and Vanderbilt. The wins were piling up so rapidly, 18 in a row, that naysayers were predicting a loss to Arkansas when the Hogs came to visit Rupp Arena on February 11. The Wildcats had never defeated the Hogs in regular season play since head coach Nolan Richardson took over in 1992.

Kentucky used the game to unveil its new denim uniforms. Early on in the game, the doubters were reveling. Arkansas grabbed a 19-9 lead with less than 13 minutes to play in the first half. The Hogs battled the Wildcats throughout the game. Finally, following a Kareem Reid layup with less than seven minutes to play, Kentucky's lead fell to three, 69-66. An Epps three-pointer sparked the Wildcats to a 16-5 run to close out the game.

The victories continued to come. Kentucky

posted a 13-point victory over Georgia, a 40-point win at Tennessee, a 19-point blasting of Alabama, a 31-point win over Florida, a 15-point victory at Auburn, and a 38-point demolition of Vanderbilt at Kentucky.

Twenty-five consecutive wins. A 16-0 report card. Amazing.

Some tagged the SEC tournament as the Kentucky Invitational in New Orleans. It began with easy victories over Florida and Arkansas. Pitino was looking for his fifth SEC tourney championship. But Mississippi State, as if it had caught lightning in a bottle, sent a wake-up call to Walker, Delk, Pope, McCarty and the rest of the team in the final game. Mississippi's 84-73 victory was another learning experience. The most important lesson? You can't underestimate anyone in post-season play.

The loss sent the Wildcats from the East region to the Midwest region and dropped Kentucky from its No. 1 ranking to No. 2. But Walker was prepared to make amends for the team's sub-par play in the conference tournament. He

The Kentucky players on the bench react glumly to the 84-73 loss to Mississippi State in the SEC Tournament, March 10, 1996. (From left are Jeff Sheppard, Antoine Walker and Ron Mercer.)

Antoine Walker dunks the ball against the defense of San José State's Marmet Williams in the 1996 NCAA playoffs.

seemed to have learned his lesson very quickly.

In his sophomore year, he had demonstrated a lot of maturity. He took better shots from the field. He did a better job of passing the ball. He played great defense. Prior to the NCAA playoffs, Walker sent a message to a lot of college basketball teams in the SEC tournament. He scored 51 points, grabbed 28 rebounds, and handed out 10 assists in three games. He was named to the all-tournament team.

Once March Madness started, Walker continued to impress the Kentucky fans with his all-around play. In the Wildcats' first two NCAA tournament victories, Walker scored 35 points, pulled down 20 rebounds, and chipped in with 10 assists and seven steals.

In the first game against San José State, he made some spectacular plays. He took a basic pass from teammate Ron Mercer while moving to the basket and turned it into a marvelous slam. On another occasion, he lofted an overhead pass to Walter McCarty for an easy layup.

"We're at our best when we're rebounding and being unselfish, getting out in the open court," Walker told the *Fort Worth Star-Telegram.* "We're a quick team. We're not a half-court team. We can execute in the half court, but we like to go up and down."

In the Virginia Tech game, he hit three pointers, scored down low, played good defense, and rebounded extremely well. He also had some great passes in the open court.

"What really ignites this team is great passing," Pitino told the *Fort Worth Press Telegram.* "We feed off that. Our guys get so excited about that. For these guys, dunks are easy. The passes that lead to the dunks are hard."

At Kentucky, Walker was playing with a host of sensational players, including McCarty and Pope, both 6'10", Delk, Anderson, and Ron Mercer. He averaged 27 minutes a game on one of the most talented teams in Kentucky's basketball history. If Pitino would have increased the time he played in each game, he certainly would have averaged more points, rebounds, and assists a game.

"I think I have the capability to do that," Walk-

Antoine Walker gives the number one sign as he and his fellow teammates celebrate their pending victory over Utah in the NCAA Midwest Regional game. From left: Antoine Walker, Anthony Epps, Jeff Shepard, Mark Pope, Walter McCarty, Derek Anderson.

A true team effort gave the Kentucky Wildcats their 1996 NCAA Championship. Here Anthony Epps, Antoine Walker, and Ron Mercer leave the floor at half time in the championship game.

er told the *Fort Worth Star-Telegram* during the Wildcats' march to the title. "We have a lot of depth and this is a fun team to play on. We have to be consistent every game. We've got guys to do that. We've got guys to rebound and play tough defense.

"Every game it's going to be somebody different. I've got to be consistent, whether it's scoring or rebounding or playing good defense. Everybody on this team serves a role. I'm not going to get 20 [points] and 10 [rebounds] every game. We're at our best when we help each other out."

Walker continued to play great basketball throughout the NCAA playoffs. In the Wildcats' 81-74 win over Massachusetts in the Final Four, he tallied 14 points, six rebounds, four assists, and four steals, including a huge steal in the second half to help seal the win. He was named to the Midwestern Region all-tournament team after scoring 28 points and grabbing 14 rebounds in Kentucky's victories over Utah and Wake Forest.

In the NCAA championship game, Walker contributed 11 points, a team-high nine rebounds and four assists as Kentucky topped Syracuse, 76-67.

In addition to Walker's contribution, Delk tied an NCAA record, hitting seven three-point shots in the game. Anderson and Pope made some big plays in the closing minutes to give Kentucky the NCAA crown. Mercer had a tremendous game coming off the bench, scoring 20 points as a freshman.

The championship was the season's biggest highlight. But there were several other great achievements by the team, including winning a school record 27 straight games, tallying 86 points in the first half against LSU, surpassing North Carolina in the all-time wins category, moving past Indiana to reassume sole possession of second place in national titles with six, and completing the SEC regular season with a 16-0 record (the first undefeated conference mark since Alabama in the 1950s). The only Kentucky losses were to final four teams Massachusetts and Mississippi State.

"Getting ready to play Kentucky is like playing a wishbone offense one time a year, like facing Sandy Koufax's fastball once in a season," Dave Odom, Wake Forest head coach, told the *Houston Chronicle* after his team lost to the Wildcats in the NCAA tournament.

Walker's no Sandy Koufax. But he was one

Antoine Walker (right) and Anthony Epps defend their way to a national title against Syracuse's Otis Hill.

of the Wildcats' big hitters. Pitino compared him to Jamal Mashburn, an ex-Kentucky Wildcat, who now plays for the Miami Heat.

"Every day, he reminds me more and more of Jamal Mashburn . . . the way he can step out and handle [the ball], make everybody better with his passing," Pitino told *USA Today*. "What I look for more than anything else is competitive drive. Sometimes, when you hear selfish basketball player, he just wants to do well. He wants the shot.

"Antoine came in and, definitely, he wanted to shine. He wanted the basketball. The one thing we convinced him of is that, 'You can shine, but in different ways.' "

Walker enjoyed being a part of the championship spotlight. He didn't let the pressure of being in the NCAA championship game at the Continental Airlines Arena in East Rutherford, New Jersey, affect his game.

Walker played well in the championship game and throughout the NCAA playoffs. He played against some fantastic players like Tim Duncan of Wake Forest, Marcus Camby of Massachusetts, Keith Van Horn of Utah, and John Wallace of Syracuse. All went on to the NBA. He had faced the major players and held his own.

Several of Walker's teammates also went on to the NBA. Walker, McCarty, and Mercer all play for Pitino in Boston. Delk plays for the Golden State Warriors, and Anderson plays for the Cleveland Cavaliers.

Pitino labeled the team "The Untouchables" after the Wildcats were crowned champions of college basketball. The title seemed very appropriate. It was a special team. And Walker had been a key member.

4

LEAVING KENTUCKY FOR THE NBA

When the Kentucky Wildcats won the NCAA championship in 1996, Rick Pitino could hardly wait for the next year to get started. That was until Pitino found out his brilliant sophomore Antoine Walker had declared himself eligible for the NBA draft. Walker joined a long list of underclassmen who left school early for the multi-million dollar contracts. Players like Marcus Camby of Massachusetts, Stephon Marbury of Georgia Tech, Allen Iverson of Georgetown, Ray Allen of Connecticut, and others.

Walker claimed his decision had a lot to do with the Wildcats winning the national championship.

"I would have been back, definitely," Walker told the *Cincinnati Enquirer*. "That was the determining factor."

Pitino, who called Walker "the straw that stirs our drink," was hoping he would stay in Lexington for another season.

Antoine Walker decided to go pro in his sophomore year and was drafted by the Boston Celtics.

"God, he would have been terrific as a junior . . . maybe [national] player of the year," Pitino told the *Cincinnati Enquirer* at Walker's press conference.

Pitino had continued to mold and shape Walker at the University of Kentucky. He had seen him grow and mature during his two years there.

"I've never enjoyed coaching a player more than him," Pitino told the Chicago *Sun-Times.* "Because even if we have a simple one-on-one shooting contest, he wants to kill the other guy. That's why I've enjoyed coaching him so much—because of his competitive nature."

Walker had had a great season, averaging 15.2 points, 8.4 rebounds, and 2.9 assists a game. In his freshman season, he was chosen most valuable player of the Southeastern Conference Tournament. As a sophomore, he received all-conference honors.

However, Walker wanted to take care of his family. He had a one-year-old daughter, Crystal, and he wanted to make life easier for his mother, Diane, and five brothers and sisters.

With his huge contract, Walker would be able to take care of his family. "I'm not in it for the money. I just want my mom to have a big house," Walker told the *Providence Journal Bulletin.* "My mom struggled for 20 years. She put me in private school. Now I want to help. I can set the foundation for my brothers and sisters to go to college."

"My family's been there for me my whole life," Walker told the *Cincinnati Enquirer.* "It's come time for me to repay them."

Walker's mother Diane wanted this to be his decision.

Antoine Walker and Rick Pitino at the news conference announcing Walker's decision to go pro.

"This is Antoine's life and his career," she told the *Cincinnati Enquirer* during her son's press conference. "[The NBA] is his dream, and I think he's ready."

Diane told the *Hartford Courant,* "Antoine always went to school. He didn't hang out in the streets, he didn't hang out at the playground. I would have preferred Antoine to stay in school. He knows how I feel about education. But

Antoine has accomplished a lot, and he's a good person. I've told him, 'Just go back and get that piece of paper for me,' and I believe he'll do that. He has never let me down."

When Walker decided to turn pro, Pitino, former New York Knicks head coach, used the opportunity to criticize the NBA's collective bargaining agreement. The agreement puts a salary cap on all rookies and limits their contracts to three years. Then it allows the players to become eligible for unrestricted free agency after that point. Basically, this means the players can make even more money.

"The whole system is out of whack," Pitino told the *Kentucky Post.* "These kids, none of them are ready for the NBA, and I can tell you that from the four years I spent [coaching in the NBA].

"But the system is such that they must go. Everybody thought the new collective bargaining agreement would stop them. It's gone the other way. They're in a rush to get the three years up so they can make the big money."

In spite of Pitino's views, he was pleased Walker was selected by the Boston Celtics. Walker was chosen with the Celtics' sixth pick in the 1996 NBA draft.

"He helped our dreams come true," said Pitino, a TNT commentator during the draft. "You saw his family crying backstage. Me and all of Kentucky are crying for other reasons: We hate to see him go."

Walker joined Tony Delk, picked No. 16 by the Charlotte Hornets, and Walter McCarty, chosen No. 19, as the sixth trio from the same school to be picked in the first round of the same draft.

Walker didn't know for sure if Boston was

going to pick him. A trade sent center Eric Montross and the team's No. 9 selection to Dallas, improving their chances of drafting Walker.

"No, I thought I'd be going to Minnesota [with the fifth pick]," Walker told the *Lexington Herald Leader.* "My people didn't think the Celtics would take me.

"It's kind of similar to the University of Kentucky. I know [Boston's] had some tough times in the last couple of years, but they still have a lot of tradition. I'm used to playing somewhere with a lot of tradition, so it should be great to play there."

Former Boston Celtic coach M. L. Carr was elated with the selection of Walker. He was very impressed with his overall skills.

"Obviously, Antoine was the man we wanted in that spot," said Carr.

"This young man has ball-handling skills, he defends, he can take the ball to the basket, and in my opinion, he's the best passing big man to come around in a while," Carr told the *Boston Herald.* "He's the entire package."

Speaking of the entire package, Walker's contract provided him and his family with a great deal of money. It's not easy for some players who come from poor families to stay in school. Today, it's rare if a player with Walker's ability remains in college for more than two years.

Walker realizes he's blessed with a lot of talent. He also realizes that there are a number of kids who can't afford to see him play.

So, Walker started a program at Boston's Fleet Center where he hosts 44 area youngsters at the Celtics' home games.

The community section is called "Antoine's

Crazy 8's." As a part of this program, each participating youngster receives tickets to the game, bus transportation, a tee shirt and a refreshment.

"It means an awful lot to me to be able to give something back to the community," Walker told the *Celtics Insider.* "I am very fortunate to be a professional basketball player playing for a legendary sports franchise. Success is winning games, winning championships, and being an all-star. Success also means the smiles, cheers, and memories that you see in the kids' faces."

The United States Postal Service recognized and awarded players from the Celtics who worked extremely hard in the community. Each month during the 1997-98 season, a player was honored for his many contributions to "Communiteam"—the Celtics' community outreach program. Walker was recognized one month as the "Communiteam" player of the month, honored for the way he set up "Antoine's Crazy 8's" and his service to other organizations.

Among the organizations he supported were: Boston Medical Center, Boston Celtics Stay in School Program, and The New England Sports Lodge. Walker also became a spokesperson for the Fleet All-Stars program, which encourages youngsters to get involved with community service projects. In addition to his community efforts with young people, Walker enjoys visiting different neighborhoods throughout the city of Boston. He takes special pride in visiting some of Boston's roughest areas, spending plenty of time, for example, speaking with Roxbury's Young Achievers in math and science. These outstanding students were given the opportunity to be a part of Walker's special community section. If it wasn't for him, the kids would not have been able to attend a Celtics' game.

Walker has worked with community organizations in other cities, too. He made a guest appearance at the opening of a restored Columbia Park playground in Providence, Rhode Island, where youngsters participated in a slam-dunk contest.

Walker also teamed up with Coca-Cola, sponsor of the Sprite NBA Backboard Program, a nationwide drive to replace the backboards in playgrounds in 12 cities across the country. Coca-Cola spent nearly $30,000 to put up green and white backboards in the Washington Park neighborhood and throughout the city. Walker's appearance was a real treat for many kids from the Washington Park Community Center.

Walker's commitment to the Boston community has a lot of do with his background. Being raised in Chicago, he knows how difficult it can be growing up in the inner city.

Although Walker didn't finish his college education and left Kentucky for the fame and fortune of the NBA, he has not forgotten his family and helping people who are less fortunate. Walker's basketball skills make him a star on the court, and his kindness and generosity make him a star off the court.

5
A ROOKIE WITH THE BOSTON CELTICS

There aren't too many big men who have joined the NBA and made the same impact as Antoine Walker. In 1996-97, he led the Boston Celtics in scoring (17.5 ppg), rebounds (9.0 rpg), and blocked shots (53). He was the only player to appear in all 82 games.

Walker was chosen to participate in the 1997 Rookie Game in Cleveland, Ohio, and he led the winning East team with 20 points. In the Rookie Game, he played with some of the league's brightest stars, including Allen Iverson of the Philadelphia 76ers, Marcus Camby of the Toronto Raptors, Stephon Marbury of the Minnesota Timberwolves, and Ray Allen of the Milwaukee Bucks.

He was the second highest rookie scorer in team history, with 1,435 points, falling behind Larry Bird's 1,745. Bird, now head coach of the Indiana Pacers, liked Walker's potential immediately.

An enthusiastic Antoine Walker celebrates a key defensive play.

"This guy is going to be a special player," said Bird, a special assistant to former Celtics head coach M. L. Carr at the time. "I like Walker and I like Allen [Iverson] a lot, too. I had those two guys ranked higher than anyone else. Sure, Iverson's a special player, but he's 6 foot."

While Iverson electrified the crowds throughout the NBA, Walker was impressive in his own way. He glided to the basket for easy scores. He displayed great range on his jumpshot. He also rebounded the ball extremely well.

Unfortunately, Boston had a terrible season his first year, and Walker was the Celtics' only bright spot during his rookie year. The Celtics finished with a horrible 15-67 record. The poor season was due to a number of injuries; the Celtic players missed a total of 471 games, more than the record 388 injuries suffered by the Los Angeles Clippers in 1987-88.

Dana Barros, who was supposed to be a starter before the season, started only eight games. He missed one game due to illness and 57 others because of a sore left ankle.

Dee Brown missed 61 games with a variety of injuries to his back, a knee, and a foot. Pervis Ellison was lost to a broken right toe eight games into the season and missed 63 games in total.

Greg Minor missed 59 games with a right foot injury. Dino Radja missed 57 games due to knee injuries.

Although David Wesley led the team with 537 assists and Rick Fox had a team-high 167 steals, Walker clearly became the team's most consistent player. Whenever the Celtics needed a big basket, the team usually looked for him.

With all the injuries, Walker certainly didn't

A collision under the hoop in an all-out effort for the rebound by rookie Boston Celtic Antoine Walker and the Milwaukee Bucks' Glenn Robinson and Andrew Lang.

let his team down. M. L. Carr, who was the Celtics' head coach at the time, ran a lot of plays for Walker. He allowed him to use his great offensive skills not only when the Celtics ran their half-court offense, but when they ran the fast-break, too.

The Celtics had a pretty good running game with Walker, Fox, Wesley, Eric Williams, and Todd Day. In fact, Williams and Day were solid contributors for Boston.

Williams led the Celtics with 328 free throws made. Day was the team leader with 126 three-pointers made.

While the veterans displayed some scoring talent, it was Walker who usually made the big shots. He wasn't afraid to connect from three-point range off the break. He also had the confidence to take the ball to the basket.

When Boston couldn't get an easy hoop off the break, they usually got the ball inside to Walker. He used his 6'9", 224-pound frame to score some points inside.

It wasn't easy to guard him close to the basket. Walker had great strength and could use his power to score against opponents in the lane. When Walker didn't use his power, he would put the ball on the floor and use his quickness to get by his defenders.

Walker played his rookie season as if the Celtics were playing for the championship. He didn't let the losing affect his game.

The Celtics' 15 wins were their fewest ever and the second fewest in the NBA during the 1996-97 season. They did not win a game against a division opponent until their final division game at Philadelphia on April 18 against the 76ers. Boston missed the playoffs for the second straight year, the first time that happened since the 1977-78 and 1978-79 seasons.

Boston is one of the most storied basketball franchises in the NBA. The team has had a number of fantastic players like Bill Russell, Bob Cousy, Sam Jones, John Havlicek, Larry Bird, Kevin

*Walker fights the defense
of 76er Scott Williams.*

McHale, and Robert Parish. There were also great
coaches like Red Auerbach and K.C. Jones.

Walker hadn't wanted to play college basketball in the Windy City, but he certainly didn't
mind playing against the hometown Chicago Bulls

Antoine Walker is difficult to guard with his great strength and drive.

once he joined the Celtics. As a kid, Walker was a big fan of the Bulls. In fact, he actually rooted for Chicago until he became a Celtic. Whenever he played at the United Center in Chicago, it was a big game for Walker. It wasn't because he was playing against the Bulls; it was because there was always plenty of family and friends watching him.

In just his first season, Walker had become a big part of the Celtics basketball history. The ex-Kentucky All-American was not used to losing basketball games. During his final season with the Wildcats, he lost just two games. Carr, Auerbach, and Bird knew that Walker was not only a great player, but a player who could help rebuild a franchise.

"The Celtics have had a lot of great players play for them, and I'm very excited to be part of a team with so much tradition," Walker told the *Boston Herald.* "This is a great opportunity for me. Hopefully, I can bring a lot of good things to this organization."

Walker did a lot of great things for the Celtics. He paced the team in field goals made, field goals attempted, offensive, defensive, and total rebounds, blocks, points, and points per game.

He was first in rebounds per game, third in points per game, steals per game, and minutes played, fourth in assists per game, and eighth in field goal percentage among all rookies.

He had scored more than 10 points 74 times, more than 10 points in each of the last 20 games, and in 27 of the last 28. The lone exception was a seven-minute outing due to a sprained right ankle.

He tallied more than 20 points on 30 occasions, more than 30 points three times, and more than 10 rebounds twice. He produced 31 double-doubles and two triple-doubles, at Philadelphia and Charlotte.

He had 40-plus minutes 38 times, including the last 14 games. Walker started 68 games, beginning on January 3 and playing to the end of the season.

For a rookie, he accomplished a lot in his first year.

6

COMMERCIAL ENDORSEMENTS

Not everyone in the NBA receives a major shoe contract or commercial endorsement. Unless, of course, your name is Michael Jordan, Grant Hill, Shaquille O'Neal, Charles Barkley, Karl Malone, Alonzo Mourning, or Tim Hardaway. They are some of the NBA's top players.

But there are also a number of young NBA players with major shoe deals and commercials, including Stephon Marbury, Kevin Garnett, Allen Iverson, and Kobe Bryant. Antoine Walker is also in this group. He was given a big sneaker contract by Adidas.

His first commercial was designed to help explain the type of basketball player Antoine was. In it, he took a very basic view of what it is like to play in the NBA.

He showed where he works (in the arena), made mention of his co-workers (teammates), called attention to his customers (the fans). The commercial ends with Walker stating, "I made

---

Though double-teamed, Walker drives for the basket during a March 1998 game against the Miami Heat.

A fight for the rebound between Walker and the New Jersey Nets' Chris Gatling.

baskets." The commercial demonstrates how Walker approaches the game of basketball.

He says he's not interested in the fame and has no desire to be a celebrity. He simply wants to come to work, work alongside his co-workers, entertain his customers, and do his job—making baskets.

Walker has received a great deal of publicity throughout his playing career. Just about everyone knew how great a player he was coming out of Chicago's Mt. Carmel High School. At 18, he was easily one of the top 20 high school players in the nation.

At Kentucky, he made an even bigger name for himself. The Wildcats became a powerhouse in college basketball over the years. On any given Saturday or Sunday afternoon from December through March, their games were on television. Walker benefited from this, receiving a tremendous amount of national recognition while playing for Kentucky.

Winning the national championship didn't hurt, either.

When Walker decided to leave Kentucky, most of the pro scouts, agents, and sneaker companies anticipated he would do well in the NBA. Adidas took the initiative and signed Walker.

The Celtics had a miserable season in Walker's rookie year, even though the ex-Kentucky standout played extremely well. Walker was sensational his second year, making the NBA All-Star team. In spite of the limited success in recent years, the Celtics still have one of the most storied basketball franchises in the NBA.

One of the most vocal players in the league, Walker has developed a reputation for talking it up on the court. He is a determined player who hopes to take his team to an NBA title.

CHRONOLOGY

1976   Antoine Devon Walker born on August 12 in Chicago, Illinois

1994   Named a high school All-American at Mt. Carmel High School in
            Chicago; signs a letter of intent to play for Kentucky

1994-95   Averages 7.8 points and 4.5 rebounds a game for the Wildcats as a
            freshman

1995-96   Averages 15.2 points and 8.4 rebounds while leading Kentucky to a
            national championship as a sophomore; selected after his sophomore
            season by the Boston Celtics in the first round, the sixth pick overall
            in the NBA draft

1996-97   Named to the NBA All-Rookie First Team; leads the Celtics
            in scoring (17.5 ppg), rebounds (9.0 rpg), and blocked shots (53) and
            is the only Celtic to appear in all 82 games; scores the second
            most points (1,435) of any rookie in Celtics history, trailing only Larry
            Bird, who had 1,745; scores a team-high 20 points and grabs
            nine rebounds in the Rookie All-Star Game

1997-98   Selected by the coaches as a reserve for the Eastern Con-
            ference in the NBA All-Star Game in New York

STATISTICS

ANTOINE WALKER

College Statistics

Season/Team	G	MIN	FG Pct	FT Pct	REB	AST	PTS	RPG	PPG
94-95 Kentucky	33	479	.419	.712	148	47	259	4.5	7.8
95-96 Kentucky	36	971	.416	.631	302	104	547	8.4	15.2
TOTALS	69	1450	.449	.660	450	151	806	6.5	11.7

NBA Statistics

Season/Team	G	MIN	FGM	FGA	Pct	FTM	FTA	Pct	REB	AST	PTS	RPG	PPG
96-97 Boston	82	2970	576	1354	.425	231	366	.631	741	262	1435	9.0	17.5
97-98 Boston	82	3268	722	1705	.423	305	473	.645	836	273	1840	10.2	22.4
TOTALS	164	6238	1298	3059	.424	536	839	.639	1577	535	3275	9.6	20.0

G	games
FGA	field goals attempted
FGM	field goals made
Pct	percent
FTA	free throws attempted
FTM	free throws made
REB	rebounds
AST	assisits
PTS	points
RPG	rebounds per game
PPG	points per game

FURTHER READING

Barnhouse, Wendell. "Kentucky's Walker Becomes Key to Team's Hopes for National Title." *Fort Worth Star-Telegram*, March 19, 1996.

Bianchine, Jim, "The Greening of the Bluegrass," *Basketball Digest*, April 1988.

Bulpett, Steve. "Walker: A Star Is Born." *Boston Herald*. January 28, 1998.

Cofman, Mark. "Walker C's New 6th Man." *Boston Herald*. June 27, 1996.

Dorsey, Matt. "Taking It to the Next Level." *Full Court Press*. January 12, 1998.

Fee, Gayle and Laura Raposa. "Antoine to Host High-Achieving Students." *Boston Herald*. January 16, 1998.

Gamble, Tom. "Pitino: Walker's Family." *Kentucky Post*. May 6, 1996.

Grant, Mike, "Walker Leads U.K.'s First Round Parade," *Louisville Courier Journal*, June 27, 1996.

Greenberg, Alan. "He Can Assist/Celtics Walker Hones Career, Helps Family." *Hartford Courant*.

Holley, Michael. "Walker Ahead of Pitino Schedule." *Boston Globe*. March 6, 1998.

May, Peter. "Walker Goes to the Celtics with 6th pick." *Boston Globe*. June 27, 1996.

May, Peter. "Walker Reaches the Stars." *Boston Globe*, January 28, 1998.

May, Peter. "He Draws Praise, Not Attention." *Boston Globe*. February 8, 1998.

Schmidt, Neil. "Goals Met, UK Soph Picks NBA." *Cincinnati Enquirer.* May 6, 1996.

Szostak, Mike. "Celts' Walker Pitches in for City's Parks." *Providence Journal-Bulletin*. May 20, 1997.

Szostak, Mike. "Walker Went Pro to Help Family." *Providence Journal-Bulletin*. June 28, 1996.

Tipton, Jerry. "Walker Gives Up Flash for UK Title Dash." *Lexington Herald Leader.* February 17, 1996.

ABOUT THE AUTHOR

Donald Hunt is a sportswriter for *The Philadelphia Tribune.* He covers high school, college, and professional sports. He is also the author of *The Philadelphia Big 5* and *Great Names in Black College Sports.*

INDEX

31